THE Little Red Hen

Retold by Jenny Giles

Illustrated by Betty Greenhatch

2

Once upon a time,
there was a little red hen.
She lived on a farm
with a duck, a dog, and a pig.

One day, she found some wheat.

"I will plant this wheat,"
said the little red hen.
"Who will help me?"

"Not I," quacked the duck,
and she went away
to swim in the pond.

"Not I," barked the dog,
and he went away
to run in the field.

"Not I," grunted the pig,
and he went away
to roll in the mud.

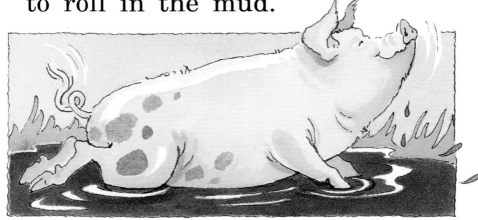

"Then I will do it myself!"
said the little red hen.
And she did.

Soon the wheat began to grow.
"I must water the wheat,"
said the little red hen.
"Who will help me?"

"Not I!" quacked the duck
from the pond.

"Not I!" barked the dog
from the field.

"Not I!" grunted the pig
from the mud.

"Then I will do it myself,"
said the little red hen.
And she did.

Soon the wheat was ready to cut.
"I must cut the wheat,"
said the little red hen.
"Who will help me?"

"Not I," quacked the duck.

"Not I," barked the dog.

"Not I," grunted the pig.

"Then I will do it myself,"
said the little red hen.
And she did.

"I must make the wheat
into flour,"
said the little red hen.
"Who will help me?"

"Not I," quacked the duck.

"Not I," barked the dog.

"Not I," grunted the pig.

"Then I will do it myself,"
said the little red hen.
And she did.

13

"I will bake some bread
with this flour,"
said the little red hen.
"Who will help me?"

"Not I," quacked the duck.

"Not I," barked the dog.

"Not I," grunted the pig.

So the little red hen
baked the bread herself.

When the bread was baked
and ready to eat,
the little red hen
took it out of the oven.

"Who will help me eat
the bread?"
asked the little red hen.

"I will!" quacked the duck,
and she came out of the pond.

"I will!" barked the dog,
and he came out of the field.

"I will!" grunted the pig,
and he came out of the mud.

17

18

"Oh, no you will **not**!"
said the little red hen.
"You did **not** help me
plant the wheat,
water the wheat,
cut the wheat,
make the flour,
or bake the bread.
So I will not let you
eat the bread."

"I will eat it myself,"
said the little red hen.

And she did!

A play
The Little Red Hen

People in the play

 Narrator

 Little Red Hen

 Duck

 Dog

 Pig

Narrator

Once upon a time,
there was a little red hen.
She lived on a farm
with a duck, a dog, and a pig.

One day she found some wheat.

Little Red Hen

I will plant this wheat.
Who will help me?

Duck

Quack-quack! Not I!
I'm going to swim in the pond.

Dog

Woof-woof! Not I!
I'm going to run in the field!

Pig

Oink-oink! Not I!
I'm going to roll in the mud!

Little Red Hen

Then I will do it myself.

Narrator

And she did.
The little red hen
planted the wheat all by herself.
Soon the wheat began to grow.

Little Red Hen

I must water the wheat.
Who will help me?

Duck

Quack-quack! Not I!
I like it here in the pond.

Dog

Woof-woof! Not I!
I like it here in the field.

Pig

Oink-oink! Not I!
I like it here in the mud.

Little Red Hen

Then I will do it myself.

Narrator

And she did.
The little red hen
watered the wheat
all by herself.
Soon the wheat was ready to cut.

Little Red Hen

I must cut the wheat.
Who will help me?

Duck

Quack-quack! Not I!

Dog

Woof-woof! Not I!

Pig

Oink-oink! Not I!

Little Red Hen

Then I will do it myself.

Narrator

And she did.
The little red hen
cut the wheat all by herself.

Little Red Hen

I must make the wheat
into flour.
Who will help me?

Duck

Quack-quack! Not I!

Dog

Woof-woof! Not I!

Pig

Oink-oink! Not I!

Little Red Hen

Then I will do it myself.

Narrator

And she did.
The little red hen
made the wheat into flour
all by herself.

Little Red Hen

I must make some bread
with this flour.
Who will help me?

Duck

Not I!

Dog

Not I!

Pig

Not I!

Little Red Hen

Then I will do it myself.

Narrator

And she did.
The little red hen
made the bread
all by herself.

Narrator

When the bread was baked
and ready to eat,
the little red hen took it
out of the oven.

Little Red Hen

Who will help me **eat** the bread?

Duck

I will! Here I come!

Narrator

And the duck came running
out of the pond.

Dog

I will! Here I come!

Narrator

And the dog came running out of the field.

Pig

I will! Here I come!

Narrator

And the pig came running out of the mud.

The little red hen looked at the duck, the dog, and the pig.

Little Red Hen

Oh, no you will **not**!
You did **not** help me
plant the wheat,
water the wheat,
cut the wheat,
make the flour,
or bake the bread.
So I will not let you
eat the bread.
I will eat it myself.

Narrator

And she did!
The little red hen
ate **all** the bread herself.